MATERIAL WORLD

Silk

Silk

by Claire Llewellyn

W

FRANKLIN WATTS
LONDON • SYDNEY

This edition 2005
Franklin Watts
96 Leonard Street
London EC2A 4XD

Franklin Watts Australia
Level 17/207 Kent Street
Sydney NSW 2000

Text copyright © Claire Llewellyn 2001

ISBN 0 7496 6372 3

Dewey Decimal
Classification Number: 677

A CIP catalogue record for this book
is available from the British Library

Series editor: Rosalind Beckman
Series designer: James Evans
Picture research: Sue Mennell
Photography: Steve Shott

Printed in China

Acknowledgements

Thanks are due to the following for kind permission to
reproduce photographs:

AKG London p. 25t
The Art Archive pp. 12 (National Gallery Budapest/Dagli Orti
(A)), 14 (Oriental Art Museum Genoa/Dagli Orti (A))
Corbis Images pp. 9t (Kevin R. Morris), 11t (Bass Museum of
Art), 13t (Christine Osborne), 15b (Earl & Nazima Kowall),
19t (Anthony Bannister; Gallo Images), 20 (Michael Freeman),
back cover 1 (Chris Hellier)
Ecoscene pp. 16-17c (Papilio/RKP)
Holt Studios p. 17r (Bob Gibbons)
James Davis Worldwide Travel Library p. 22
NHPA p. 18 (A.N.T.)
Oxford Scientific Films p. 19b (G.I. Bernard)
Science Photo Library pp. 9b (David Parker), 21 both (Pascal
Goetgheluck)
Still Pictures pp. 26 (Shehzad Noorani), 27 (Ron Giling)

Thanks are also due to John Lewis for their help with this
project, and to Liberty and Emma Zucker for lending items
for photography.

Contents

Words printed in **bold italic** are explained in the glossary.

What is silk?

Silk is one of the world's most beautiful materials and is used to make fine things. Some materials, such as paper and glass, are cheap to make and widely used. Silk is not like these. It is expensive to produce and only used to make very special things.

Made of silk

All the things in these pictures are made of silk. Can you name them all?

Material words

Which of these words describe silk?

cold   thick   shiny

sticky stretchy

solid

heavy   stiff

dull soft strong

hard warm

hard-wearing

spongy light

crisp

colourful

rough

smooth

thin

bendy slimy

springy

runny

squashy

Fantastic fact

Silk is a kind of *fibre*. Cotton, linen, paper and wool are other materials made of fibres.

Silk shimmers with colour and light

One of the reasons why people love silk is because it is shiny and shimmery. It catches the light in a special way.

Catching the light

When rays of light hit an object, they bounce back off again. This is called **reflection**. Silk reflects light in a special way. This is because each fibre is shaped like a triangle and acts like a prism. A prism makes light sparkle and shine.

As silk catches the light, it shines beautifully.

Pure colour

Silk is soft and very **absorbent**. It soaks up **dye** like a sponge. Every dye looks good on silk - from the palest colours to the deepest, richest dyes that seem to sparkle like jewels.

Painting on silk is a craft in China. The artists need great skill because silk absorbs paint very quickly.

Try this

Take a triangular piece of glass called a prism, and place it in the sunlight. What happens to the light? Silk fibres are triangular, too, so they reflect light in the same way.

9

Silk is warm- and cool !

Silk feels light and comfortable next to the skin. It keeps you warm in winter and cool in summer.

Keeping heat out

Silk is wonderful to wear when it is hot. In India, many women wear silk saris. Saris are dresses made of one piece of silk wound loosely around the body. The Sun's heat does not easily pass through the silk. This helps to keep people cool.

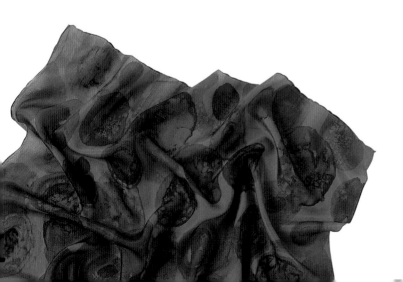

Keeping heat in

Some materials such as cotton allow heat to pass through them very easily; silk does not. Silk socks, underwear, and the lining in gloves lock in the body's heat. The silk traps a layer of warm air next to the skin. This helps to keep you warm.

Silk was once used to make tapestries. These were hung on the walls of large, draughty rooms and helped to keep out the cold.

The finest gloves are lined with silk. This makes them feel soft and warm on the skin.

Fantastic fact

Explorers in the coldest parts of the world often wear silk next to their skin.

Silk is strong and hard-wearing

Silk thread is so strong that it is used to make rugs and carpets. It is also **woven** into strong silk cloth and used in all sorts of ways.

As light as air

Parachutes and hot air balloons were once made of silk. The silk canopy was light enough to float in the air, but strong enough to take the push of the air inside it. Also, the silk folded up small and was light to carry.

The first hot air balloons were made of silk because it is both light and strong.

Taking the wear

Silk thread does not rot and is so long-lasting that it can be used to make carpets and rugs. The silk threads are knotted very tightly together to make a rug that is not only soft but also very hard-wearing.

This silk carpet has a rich pattern, built up of different colour threads.

Try this

Look at some pieces of silk thread, cotton thread and wool yarn. Which of the three is the finest? Now try pulling each of them as hard as you can. Do any of them break?

Silk is a luxury

Silk is an expensive material to produce. This is why it has always sold for very high prices. Even today, it is usually only worn at parties, weddings and on other special days.

A royal cloth

Silk takes a lot of time and effort to produce. For many years it was worn only by rich and powerful people such as emperors, princes and queens. Today, some kinds of silk are made more cheaply, and so more people can afford to wear it.

This 300-year-old Japanese *kimono* is made of silk, stitched with gold thread.

Queen for a day

Because silk is such a luxury, many women wear it on their wedding day. They feel this is one day when they deserve to wear the best!

In many countries brides wear a white or cream silk dress on their wedding day. Sometimes the veil is also made of silk.

The story of silk

It is said that the first person who made silk was a Chinese empress who lived 5,000 years ago. The method for making silk became China's great secret and was guarded for 3,000 years.

Many Chinese couples still wear traditional silk clothes on their wedding day.

Fantastic fact

Merchants who wanted to buy silk had to travel all the way to China. The silk was so expensive it was paid for with gold and precious stones.

Silk is made by silkworms

Silk is a **natural** material. It is made from the long, silky fibres produced by silkworms. The silkworm is not really a worm, but the caterpillar of the silk moth.

Natural silk

There are many different kinds of silkworm and most of them live in the wild. All silkworms can make silk, but most of it is brown or of poor quality. The very best silk is made by the caterpillar of the *Bombyx* silk moth. Today, the *Bombyx* silk moth only lives on farms.

1 The moth lays its eggs.

4 The adult moth crawls out of the cocoon and flies off.

Farming silkworms

Silk farmers look after their silkworms with great care. At every stage of life, they are kept spotlessly clean and protected from *disease*.

A silk moth goes through four different stages as it grows. These four stages are called its life cycle.

2 Each egg hatches into a caterpillar, which feeds and grows.

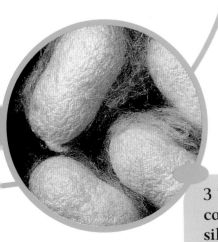

3 The fully-grown caterpillar spins a silk *cocoon*. Inside, its body changes. It is called a *pupa*.

Fantastic fact

Spiders also make silk, which they use to build shelters and webs. But only the silkworm produces a glossy fibre that is strong enough to be wound up, woven and dyed.

From eggs to cocoons

Most of the world's silk is produced on farms in China, India and Japan. The silk is made from the long, sticky fibre that silkworms use to build their cocoon.

Looking after the eggs

The *Bombyx* silk moth lays its eggs in early summer. On farms the eggs are tested for disease and stored in a refrigerator. In spring they are moved to a warm room where they hatch after two to three weeks.

Silkworms are dark when they first hatch. They turn white as they grow larger.

Feeding the silkworms

Young silkworms are very fussy eaters. They feed only on the leaves of mulberry trees, which are grown in **plantations** on the farm. The silkworms eat greedily. After about a month they are plump and white, and ready to make a cocoon.

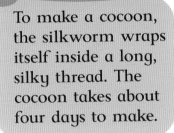

This cocoon has been cut open to show the pupa inside.

To make a cocoon, the silkworm wraps itself inside a long, silky thread. The cocoon takes about four days to make.

Fantastic fact

A silkworm's cocoon is made of one strand of silk up to 2 km long.

The silk cocoon

To make a cocoon, the silkworm squirts liquid out of its **spinneret** - a hole in its lower lip. In the air, the liquid hardens into a fine silk thread. The silk is coated with a gum called **sericin**, which binds the cocoon together.

19

From cocoons to silk

The silky cocoons are unravelled and the thread is wound on to reels. The silk is then sent to silk mills where it is woven and dyed.

Killing the pupae

The finished cocoons are plunged into hot water to kill the pupae inside. If the insects were left to develop, they would change into moths. They would bite their way out of the cocoons and break the long silk thread. Some adult moths are allowed to develop in order to lay the next batch of eggs.

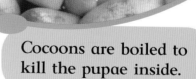

Cocoons are boiled to kill the pupae inside.

Unwinding the cocoons

The hot water washes away some of the sericin. This makes it easier to unwind the silk. Silk-workers gather the strands from several cocoons and fix them to a reeling machine. The machine unravels the cocoons, twists the strands together and winds the yarn on to a reel.

The threads of several cocoons are twisted together to make a yarn.

Raw silk

At this stage the silk yarn is known as raw silk. It is taken off the reels and twisted into bundles called *skeins*. These are shipped to silk mills all over the world.

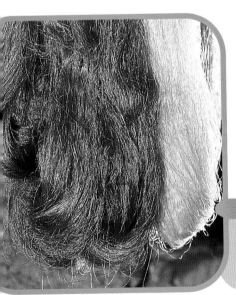

These two skeins of raw silk come from different types of silk moth. Raw silk feels coarse because it still contains some sericin.

Fantastic fact

It takes 110 cocoons to make a silk tie, 630 cocoons to make a blouse and 3,000 cocoons to make a kimono.

At the silk mill

At the silk mill, the raw silk is woven into different kinds of cloth. Most of the silk is dyed after weaving, though some of it is dyed before it is woven.

A weaver at his loom: he is holding a shuttle, the small tool that is used to weave the cloth.

Making the cloth

The raw silk is woven into cloth on machines called *looms*. Different ways of weaving, and different thicknesses of yarn, produce many different kinds of silk. After weaving, the cloth is washed to remove all the sticky sericin. This leaves a soft, smooth, cream-coloured cloth.

Printing the cloth

The woven silk is wound on to rolls called bolts. The next step is to dye the cloth or print it with a pattern.

This picture shows some of the different types of silk.

1 *Chiffon* is a very light silk that you can see through.

2 *Satin* is soft and very smooth.

3 *Shot silk* is woven with two different colours. This makes it shimmer in the light.

4 *Brocade* is a heavy, woven silk.

5 *Organza* is a stiff, see-though silk.

6 *Dupion silk* has a soft, bumpy feel.

Woven silk

Sometimes the skeins of silk are dyed before weaving. The yarns are wound on to reels that can be used on special weaving looms. These create the pattern as they weave the cloth, using up to eight different colours at a time.

Fantastic fact

Silk can also be knitted by machine. Knitted silk is very fine. It is used to make sweaters, underwear and linings for gloves.

Artificial silk

Silk is so expensive that scientists have tried to copy it. The 'silk' they have invented is not made by silkworms. It is made from chemicals instead.

'Silk' from oil

Artificial silk is made from the chemicals in oil, which scientists use to make plastic. When the plastic is melted and forced through tiny holes (just as natural silk is forced through a silkworm's spinneret), it produces long threads that harden as they cool. These threads can be woven into artificial silk.

Polyester is soft and shiny like silk, but much cheaper and easier to care for.

One of these scarves is made of silk. Can you guess which one? (The answer is on page 30.)

24

New materials

There are many different kinds of artificial silk. *Nylon* was first made about 60 years ago. It was used instead of silk to make stockings and thread. Since then, other new fibres have been invented, such as *polyester*. Artificial fibres absorb dyes well, and are comfortable and keep their shape. Yet none of them has quite the look or feel of natural silk.

Mein Strumpf bleibt Bemberg

This German advertisement for nylon stockings appeared in the 1930s, when nylon was still very new.

Try this

Find two similar items - one made of natural silk, the other made of an artificial silk. Ask your friends to feel and look at the two items carefully. Can they tell which one is which?

Silk farming

Silk farming does not damage the **environment** with **pollution** or waste. It provides work and money for millions of farmers in China and the **Far East**.

Silk is a small industry

Silk farming takes a lot of skill, time and effort. Because of this, it is quite a small industry. About 50,000 tonnes of raw silk are made every year, compared to many millions of tonnes of cotton. Silk farming has not harmed our environment.

This woman is picking mulberry leaves. The whole family can help on the silk farm.

Silk is environmentally friendly

Silk farming does not use a great deal of **energy**. Nor does it cause pollution. Silk is produced from silk moth eggs and mulberry leaves. These are renewable **raw materials**, which means that we can use them without damaging the environment.

Silk provides work

Silk farming provides a great deal of work in some of the poorer countries in the Far East. There are ten million silk farmers in China alone. Most of them produce silk alongside other kinds of farming. The silk helps farmers to earn more money without the need for expensive machines.

For many people, silk farming is a way of earning extra money.

Glossary

Absorbent	Able to soak up water and dyes.
Artificial	Not natural; made by people.
Cocoon	The silky case that a silkworm spins when it is ready to change into a moth.
Disease	An illness or infection.
Dye	A strongly coloured substance that is used to add colour to silk.
Energy	The power that makes machines and living things able to work.
Environment	All the world around us, including the land, the air and the sea.
Far East	A part of the continent of Asia that contains many countries, including China and Japan.
Fibre	A long, fine thread.
Kimono	A long, loose Japanese robe.
Loom	A machine for weaving cloth.
Natural	Found in the world around us.
Nylon	A kind of artificial silk.

Plantation	A piece of land that is used to grow one type of plant such as mulberry trees.
Pollution	Spoiling the air, land or water with harmful substances.
Polyester	A kind of artificial silk.
Pupa	The stage in a silkworm's life when it develops inside a cocoon. (Plural: pupae)
Raw materials	The natural materials that are used to make something new.
Reflection	The way light bounces off something and into our eyes.
Sericin	A sticky gum on the natural silk thread that binds the cocoon together.
Skein	A bundle of silk or other kind of yarn.
Spinneret	The hole on a silkworm's lip that squirts out silk.
Woven	Describes a cloth made by passing threads over and under one another.

Index

Answer to question on page 24: the top scarf is made of silk.